MY FIRST
CHRISTMAS
ACTIVITY
B·O·O·K

ANGELA WILKES

Stoddart

A Dorling Kindersley Book

For Sam, Rose, and Cathy

Designer Jane Bull
Photographer Dave King
Home Economist Jane Suthering

Editor Stella Love
Text Designer Martin Wilson
Managing Editor Jane Yorke
Managing Art Editor Chris Scollen
Production Paola Fagherazzi

First published in Canada in 1994
by Stoddart Publishing Co. Limited,
34 Lesmill Road, Toronto, Canada M3B 2T6

First published in Great Britain in 1994
by Dorling Kindersley Limited,
9 Henrietta Street, London WC2E 8PS

Canadian Cataloguing in Publication Data.

Wilkes, Angela
My first Christmas activity book

ISBN 0-7737-2776-0

1. Christmas decorations - Juvenile literature.
2. Christmas cookery - Juvenile literature.
3. Handicraft - Juvenile literature. I. Title.

TT900.C4W5 1994   j745.594'12   C94-930438-7

Colour reproduction by Colourscan, Singapore
Printed and bound in Italy by L.E.G.O.

Dorling Kindersley would like to thank the following for
their help in producing this book: Christopher Branfield,
Jonathan Buckley, Helen Drew, Cathy McTavey,
Emma Patmore, Selena Singh, and Phoebe Thoms.

CONTENTS

CHRISTMAS IN PICTURES

My First Christmas Activity Book is full of inventive ideas for things to make for the festive season. Step-by-step photographs and simple instructions will show you how to create all kinds of sparkling decorations and seasonal gifts from everyday materials. There are also lots of recipes for delicious things to eat. On the opposite page is a list of things to read before you start, and below are the main points to look for in each project.

How to use this book

The things you need
All the ingredients or materials for each project are shown, to help you check you have everything you need.

Equipment
These photographic checklists show you which utensils or equipment you need for each project.

Step by step
Step-by-step photographs and clear instructions show you what to do at each stage of every recipe or project.

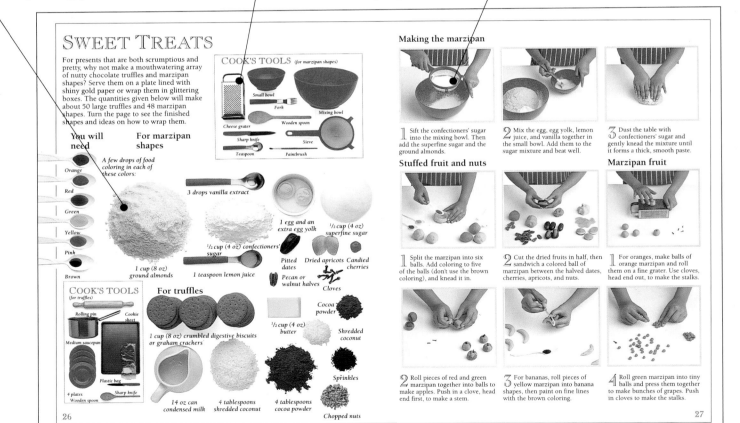

SWEET TREATS

For presents that are both scrumptious and pretty, why not make a mouthwatering array of nutty chocolate truffles and marzipan shapes? Serve them on a plate lined with shiny gold paper or wrap them in glittering boxes. The quantities given below will make about 50 large truffles and 48 marzipan shapes. Turn the page to see the finished shapes and ideas on how to wrap them.

COOK'S TOOLS (for marzipan shapes)
Small bowl · Cheese grater · Fork · Wooden spoon · Mixing bowl · Sharp knife · Sieve · Teaspoon · Paintbrush

You will need

For marzipan shapes

A few drops of food coloring in each of these colors:
Orange · Red · Green · Yellow · Pink · Brown

3 drops vanilla extract

1 cup (8 oz) ground almonds
½ cup (4 oz) confectioners' sugar
1 teaspoon lemon juice
1 egg and an extra egg yolk
½ cup (4 oz) superfine sugar
Pitted dates · Dried apricots · Candied cherries
Pecan or walnut halves · Cloves

COOK'S TOOLS (for truffles)
Rolling pin · Cookie sheet · Medium saucepan · Plastic bag · Sharp knife · 4 plates · Wooden spoon

For truffles

1 cup (8 oz) crumbled digestive biscuits or graham crackers
14 oz can condensed milk
4 tablespoons shredded coconut
4 tablespoons cocoa powder
Cocoa powder
½ cup (4 oz) butter
Shredded coconut
Sprinkles
Chopped nuts

Making the marzipan

1. Sift the confectioners' sugar into the mixing bowl. Then add the superfine sugar and the ground almonds.

2. Mix the egg, egg yolk, lemon juice, and vanilla together in the small bowl. Add them to the sugar mixture and beat well.

3. Dust the table with confectioners' sugar and gently knead the mixture until it forms a thick, smooth paste.

Stuffed fruit and nuts

1. Split the marzipan into six balls. Add coloring to five of the balls (don't use the brown coloring), and knead it in.

2. Cut the dried fruits in half, then sandwich a colored ball of marzipan between the halved dates, cherries, apricots, and nuts.

Marzipan fruit

1. For oranges, make balls of orange marzipan and roll them on a fine grater. Use cloves, head end out, to make the stalks.

2. Roll pieces of red and green marzipan together into balls to make apples. Push in a clove, head end first, to make a stem.

3. For bananas, roll pieces of yellow marzipan into banana shapes, then paint on fine lines with the brown coloring.

4. Roll green marzipan into tiny balls and press them together to make bunches of grapes. Push in cloves to make the stalks.

26

27

Things to remember

1 Read the instructions before you start, and gather together everything you will need. Put on an old apron or shirt.

2 Do not cook anything unless there is an adult there to help you.

3 Weigh or measure all the ingredients you need before starting to cook.

4 Always wear oven mitts when picking up hot dishes, or when putting things into or taking them out of the oven.

5 Be very careful with sharp knives and tools. Always ask an adult to help you use them.

6 When you are finished, always put everything away and clean up any mess.

The oven mitt symbol
Whenever you see this symbol by a picture or instruction, it means that you should ask an adult to help you.

The final results
The final picture shows you what the finished projects should look like, making it easy for you to copy them.

Perfect presents
Many of the projects would make good presents. To find out how to wrap them, turn to pages 44 to 48.

TRUFFLES AND BONBONS

Chocolate truffles

1 Melt the butter in a saucepan over low heat. Then remove the pan from the heat and let the butter cool slightly.

2 Break the biscuits into a plastic bag and fasten it. Then roll the rolling pin over the bag, crushing the biscuits into crumbs.

3 Add the biscuits, condensed milk, cocoa powder, and coconut to the melted butter, then mix everything together.

4 Spoon the mixture onto a buttered, shallow tin, then spread it out and level it with a spoon. Put it in the fridge to set.

5 Cut the mixture into 1½ in. (4 cm) squares with a knife. Then roll each square into a ball between your fingers.

6 Put the cocoa, sprinkles, nuts, and coconut on separate plates. Divide the truffles into four groups. Roll each group in a different plate.

The finished truffles

Shiny gold paper doily

Truffle coated in chocolate sprinkles

For another gift idea, fill a transparent tube with chocolate truffles. Add a festive touch to the tubes with pieces of shiny gold paper and colored ribbons.

Cocoa-coated truffle

Nutty truffle

Coconut truffle

CHOCOLATE TRUFFLES
Put the truffles in candy papers. For a special Christmassy effect you can make star-shaped doilies out of shiny gold paper and arrange your truffles on them.

Gift box containing chocolate truffles and marzipan fruit

MARZIPAN TREATS
This tempting display of marzipan treats is arranged on a gold paper doily decorated with diamonds of brightly colored foil.

Marzipan grapes

Marzipan orange

Marzipan bananas

Marzipan-stuffed apricot

Marzipan-stuffed pecan nuts

Marzipan-stuffed candied cherry

Marzipan-stuffed date

Marzipan apple

28

29

ADVENT CALENDAR

One of the best ways to enjoy the excitement of the Christmas season is to make an advent calendar. Advent is a name for the time before Christmas and an advent calendar has a surprise door for you to open on each of the 24 days leading up to Christmas Day. Make the calendar in November so that it is ready for December 1. Below you can see what you will need to make the calendar. You will need an adult's help. Turn the page to see what it will look like!

EQUIPMENT

Jar of water

Scissors

Black marker

Paintbrush

Pencil

Clear tape

Craft knife

Ruler

You will need

Blue paper

Poster paints

Red

Green

Yellow

White

Glue stick

Red ribbon

White cardboard

What to do

1 On blue paper, measure out and draw a rectangle the size you want the advent calendar to be. Carefully cut out the rectangle.

2 Place the blue rectangle on top of the white cardboard. Draw around it and cut out the matching rectangle of white cardboard.

3 In pencil, draw a picture with a Christmas theme on the blue paper. It is best to make the picture simple with bold outlines.

4 Paint your picture with poster paints. Paint one color at a time and wash the brush between each color.

5 Pencil in 24 door flaps. Make one door flap bigger than the others. Write 24 on it in marker. Number the other flaps 1 to 23.

6 Line the picture up on top of the white cardboard. Ask an adult to score along three sides of each door flap with a craft knife.

7 Lift the blue paper off the cardboard and you will see the door flaps marked out. Paint a tiny picture in each rectangle.

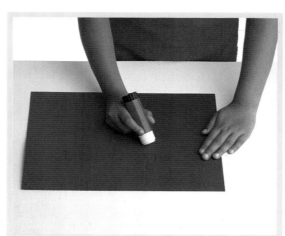

8 Turn the blue paper over so the picture is face down. Spread glue over the back of it, avoiding the door flaps.

9 Glue the white cardboard, picture-side down, to the blue paper. Make sure all the edges line up.

COUNTDOWN TO CHRISTMAS

And here is the advent calendar. On the first day of December, you can open the first door. Open door number two on the 2nd day of December, door number three on the 3rd, and so on until the 24th day, Christmas Eve, when you can open the biggest door. If you have brothers and sisters, take turns opening the doors. Behind each door there will be a surprise picture. And when there are no more doors left, you will know that it's Christmas at last!

Finishing the calendar

Cut a short piece of ribbon and tape the two ends to the back of the advent calendar to make a hanging loop, as shown.

Opening the doors

Check what the date is, then open the door with the right number on it. Carefully fold it to one side of the picture so it stays open.

The calendar will look more finished if you paint a border around the edge, like this.

Try painting pictures of toys, Christmas decorations, bells, holly, a tree, and presents.

It doesn't matter where you put the doors, as long as they are spread evenly around the calendar.

Ribbon loop for hanging the calendar

Keep the surprise pictures simple so that they stand out.

Make a big double-door for December 24th and place it in the center of the calendar.

9

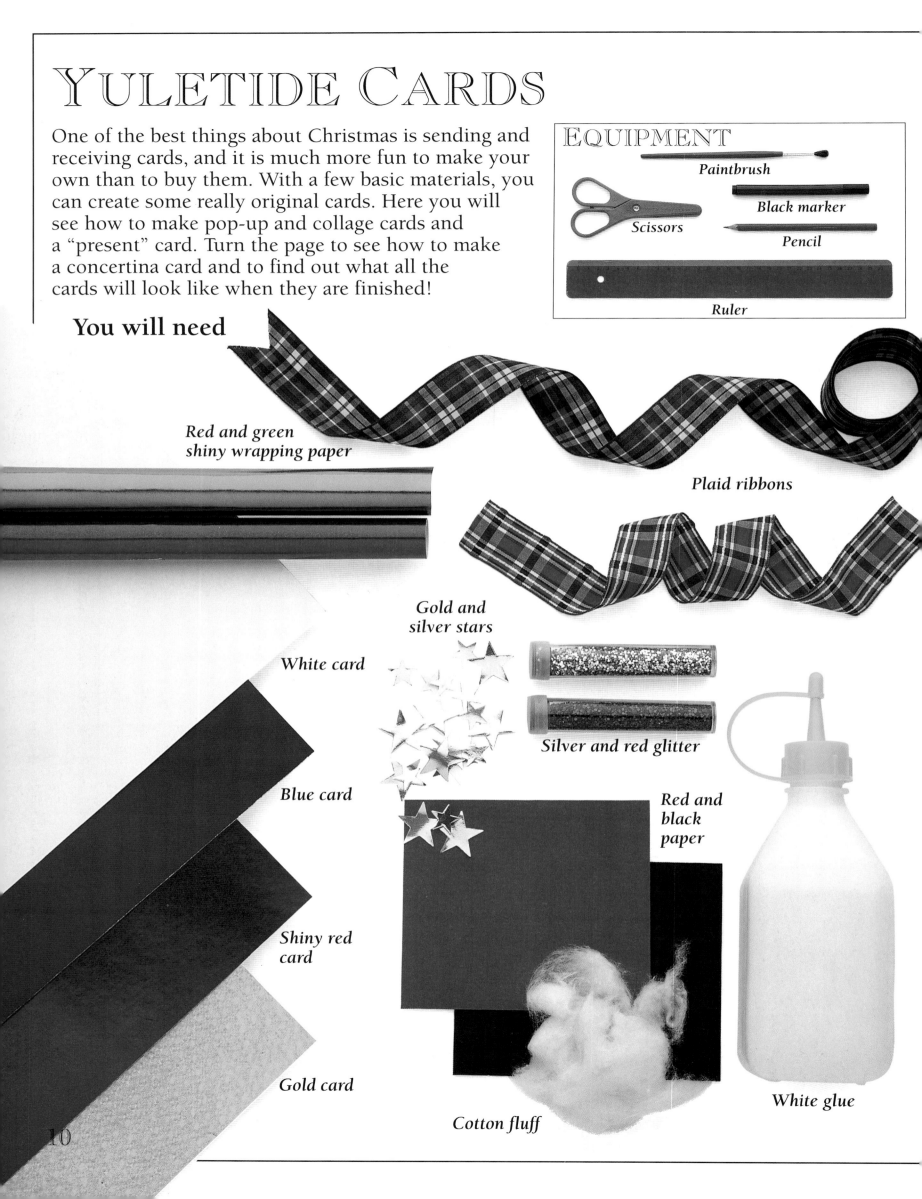

YULETIDE CARDS

One of the best things about Christmas is sending and receiving cards, and it is much more fun to make your own than to buy them. With a few basic materials, you can create some really original cards. Here you will see how to make pop-up and collage cards and a "present" card. Turn the page to see how to make a concertina card and to find out what all the cards will look like when they are finished!

You will need

Red and green
shiny wrapping paper

Plaid ribbons

Gold and
silver stars

White card

Silver and red glitter

Blue card

Red and
black
paper

Shiny red
card

Gold card

Cotton fluff

White glue

10

Smiling snowman card

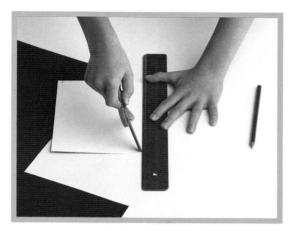

1 Cut out a rectangle of blue card. Measure halfway across it and score a line down the middle. Fold the card along the line.

2 Draw a snowman shape with glue on the front of the card and stick cotton to it. Stick some stars in the sky behind it.

3 Glue on a scarf made of ribbon and a hat, mouth, and nose made of red paper. Stick on black paper circles for eyes.

Pop-up reindeer card

1 Cut a rectangle of gold card. Score and fold it as before, then draw a reindeer inside the card, standing on the fold.

2 Carefully cut around the reindeer, but not around the bottom of its hooves.* Fold the card so the reindeer pops up.

3 Glue shiny red paper to half the card. Make a brick pattern on it with glue and glitter. Add a glitter nose and a black paper eye.

Christmas present card

1 Cut out a rectangle of red shiny card. Measure halfway across it and score a line down the middle. Fold the card in half.

2 Write a greeting inside the card. Cut out a little tag and write on it who the card is for and who it is from.

3 Tie a ribbon around the card to make it look like a present. and tie on the tag. Fasten the ribbon with a bow.

*Ask an adult to help you cut out the reindeer.

Season's Greetings

And here are the finished cards! You might try making some like this, or experiment with ideas of your own by changing the themes. Angels, Santa, bells, candles, and holly leaves and berries are other good subjects for cards. Don't forget to write your Christmas greeting in each card when it is finished, and to say who the card is from.

Concertina Christmas tree

1 Cut out a 4 in. x 5 in. (10 cm x 12 cm) rectangle of white card. Score a line down the middle of the card and fold it in half.

2 Cut a 4 in. x 16 in. (10 cm x 40 cm) strip of shiny green paper. Fold it into pleats 2 in. (5 cm) wide, as shown.

3 Draw half a tree on the top fold of paper. The branches must go over the side of the paper. Cut out the tree.

4 Open the paper out to make a row of trees. Glue the first tree to the inside of the card. Fold the other trees inside the card.

5 Cut another tree out of shiny green paper. Glue it to the front of the card, then stick on stars for decoration.

Glue one Christmas tree to the front of the card.

Gold and silver stars

CONCERTINA CHRISTMAS TREE

Glue one end of the row of trees inside the card.

SENDING THE CARDS

Buy envelopes the right size for each card, or make them out of colored paper. Fold the concertina Christmas tree inside the card before putting it in an envelope, and fold back the pop-up reindeer.

POP-UP REINDEER CARD

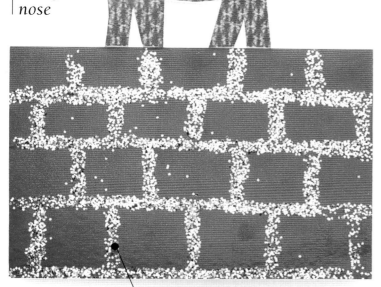

Give the reindeer a big pair of antlers when you cut it out.

Red glitter nose

Glitter is glued to shiny red paper to look like a chimney top.

CHRISTMAS PRESENT CARD

Plaid ribbon

Gift tag says who the card is for and who it is from.

SMILING SNOWMAN CARD

Plaid ribbon scarf

Cotton snow

13

CHRISTMAS COOKIES

This recipe is for delicious honey-and-spice cookies, which can be cut into festive shapes and decorated with nuts, cherries, and icing. You can buy special Christmas cutters to make the cookies, or trace the cookies on the next pages onto some cardboard and use the shapes as templates. The recipe makes about 36 cookies.

You will need

Baking sheet

Wire rack

Mixing bowl

Plastic bag

2 greaseproof icing bags

Saucepan

Small bowl

Sieve

Wooden spoon

Cookie cutters

Rolling pin

2 teaspoons

Sharp knife

Fork

Narrow spatula

For decoration

$1^{1}/_{2}$ cups (12 oz) plain flour

1 teaspoon ground cinnamon

1 teaspoon ground ginger

1 teaspoon baking soda

6 tablespoons dark brown sugar

A pinch of ground cloves

$^{1}/_{2}$ cup (4 oz) butter

1 egg

4 tablespoons honey

1 egg white

Candied cherries

Blanched almonds

Slivered almonds

Red food coloring

Narrow ribbons

1 teaspoon lemon juice

1 cup (8 oz) confectioners' sugar

14

Making the cookies

1 Grease the baking sheet and
  set the oven to 375°F/190°C.
Melt the butter, sugar, and honey
together over low heat.

2 Beat the egg. Sift the flour,
  spices, and baking soda
together, then stir in the butter
mixture and the beaten egg.

3 Mix everything together, then
  knead it into a ball of dough.
Put the dough in a plastic bag and
refrigerate it for 30 minutes.

Icing the cookies

4 Roll the dough out on a
  floured table. Flour the cutter,
then cut out dough shapes and
place them on the baking sheet.*

5 Press cherries and nuts into
  the shapes. Bake the shapes
for 15 minutes or until firm. Put
the cookies on a wire rack to cool.

1 Beat the egg white in a bowl
  with a fork for one minute. Sift
in the confectioners' sugar, add the
lemon juice, and mix until smooth.

2 For red icing, pour a quarter
  of the icing into a small bowl.
Add a few drops of red coloring
and mix until the color is even.

3 Spread the red icing evenly
  over some of the cookies with
a spatula. Cover other cookies with
an even coating of white icing.

4 Fill one icing bag with white
  icing and the other with red,
then carefully pipe patterns onto
the finished cookies.

Make holes in the tops of those cookies you want to hang.

COOKIE COLLECTION

Decorated with nuts and cherries and piped with white and red icing, the cookies make a stunning collection of decorations. Try making stars, bells, jolly snowmen, angels, and a bearded Santa. Thread ribbons through the hole in the top of each cookie to hang them on your Christmas tree. You can even make a really big cookie or two to hang on a wall or door as a special decoration.

Blanched almond

Red ribbon

STAR OF BETHLEHEM

White piping

Candied cherry

RED SANTA

White piping

Red icing

JOLLY SNOWMAN

Red piping

White icing

CHRISTMAS TREE

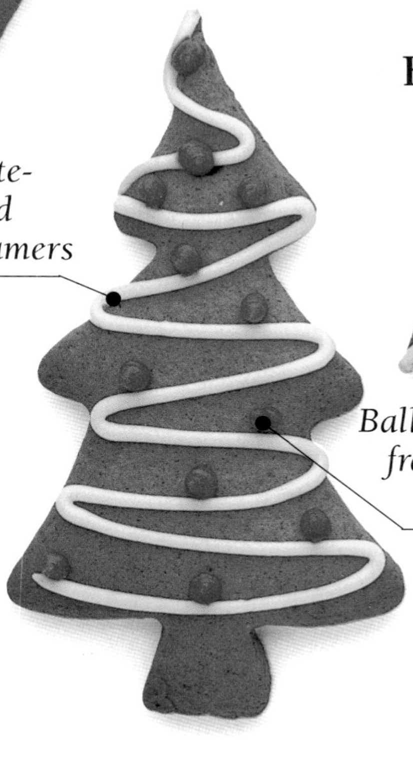

White-piped streamers

HOLLY

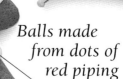

Balls made from dots of red piping

HEART

Slivered almonds

White-piped dots

Candied cherry

YULETIDE BELL

Red ribbon

Candied cherries

Blanched almonds

White piping

White piping

LITTLE ANGEL

White piping

White piping

Candied cherry

Red-piped nose

RUDOLF

SANTA'S REINDEER

Red ribbon

TWINKLING STAR

White piping

White piping

CHRISTMAS NATURE TABLE

You can make wonderful Christmas decorations and presents with things that you find outdoors, in parks, woods, and gardens. In the autumn, start looking for interesting leaves, seedheads, and berries. (Check with an adult to be sure they are not poisonous.) Display them on a nature table and then, as Christmas approaches, transform them into yuletide wreaths. Here you can find out how to make different wreaths and on the next page, you can see the finished projects.

EQUIPMENT

Paintbrush

Scissors

You will need

Red-brown leaves

Dried hydrangea flowers

Red berries

Small rosehips

Large rosehips

Other berries

Wide green and red ribbons

Gold poster paint

Interesting seedheads

Straight twigs

Fine wire

Ivy leaves

Wreath bases

Holly leaves

Lots of yew sprigs

Evergreen leaves

Traditional wreath

1 Strip the needles from the ends of the yew sprigs. Push the ends of the sprigs into the wreath base, covering the top and sides.

2 Next, bind small bundles of berries and ivy or holly leaves together. Wind wire tightly around the stems to hold them.

3 Push the berries and leaves into the wreath base to finish the wreath, then loop a wide ribbon through the back of it.

Gilded wreath

1 Paint some ivy leaves, dried hydrangea flowers, and interesting seedheads with gold poster paint. Let them dry.

2 Strengthen any weak leaf or flower stem by binding a short piece of wire along each stem with a longer piece of wire.

3 Wind a broad green ribbon around a wreath base, as shown, and tie it in a big bow at the bottom of the wreath.

Christmas bundle

4 Push the golden leaves, flowers, and seedheads into the spaces between the ribbon. Arrange them to look pretty.

1 Arrange some plain twigs into a butterfly-shaped bundle. Then bind the stems of leafy twigs and red berries to the bundle with wire.

2 Tie a red ribbon around the middle of the bundle, leaving the ends loose. Tie another ribbon around it to make a bow.

FESTIVE WREATHS

Rich in color and festive with berries and ribbons, the finished wreaths will last for several weeks, especially if they are displayed in a cool place. Just before Christmas, hang a wreath on the front door of your home as a traditional sign of welcome, or hang one on an indoor window, or above a mantelpiece as a special decoration. Try copying the wreaths shown here or create one of your own.

CHRISTMAS BUNDLE

This arrangement does not require a wreath base and can be made with any interesting leaves and berries you find.

Dried hydrangea flowers painted gold

GILDED WREATH

Based on a simple color scheme of green and gold, this wreath is very easy to create and makes a pretty Christmas decoration.

Gold poppy seedhead

Ivy leaves painted gold

Broad green ribbon

Twigs

Different kinds of leaves

Red ribbon

Red berries

TRADITIONAL WREATH
Using traditional Christmas holly leaves together with yew branches, ivy, and red berries, this wreath would look magnificent on any front door.

Red ribbon to hang the wreath

Red berries

Yew branches

Beach plums have been used here.

Large rosehips

Variegated holly leaves

Ivy leaves

Small rosehips

CHRISTMAS SCENTS

Here you can find out how to make wonderful scented gifts for Christmas: orange and lime pomanders studded with cloves, and woodland potpourri – a fragrant mixture of leaves, spices, and pinecones. To allow the scents to develop, it is best to make the potpourri about two months before Christmas. Make the pomanders two to three weeks before you need them. Turn the page to see what they look like.

EQUIPMENT

Paper bag

Scissors

Darning needle

Tape

Large jar with lid

Small bowl

Big bowl

Vegetable peeler

You will need

For the pomanders

Gold string

Green gift ribbon

Kumquats

Lime

Thin-skinned oranges

1 tablespoon ground allspice or cinnamon

1 tablespoon ground orrisroot*

Cloves

Making a pomander

1 Make holes in the fruit with a darning needle, then stick cloves in the holes so that the clove heads almost touch.

2 Mix the spice and ground orrisroot together in a small bowl and roll the fruit in it so it is coated with the powder.

3 Tie a ribbon around the fruit. Then put the fruit in a paper bag, seal the bag with tape and leave it for two to three weeks.

22   * You can buy ground orrisroot at herbalists, or health food or perfume shops.

For the potpourri

1 lemon

1 orange

Fragrant evergreen sprigs

1 oz (30 g) allspice berries

1 tablespoon ground orrisroot

Nutmegs

2 oz (55 g) star anise

Small pinecones

¹/₂ oz (15 g) whole cloves

1 tablespoon ground nutmeg

1 tablespoon ground cloves

1 tablespoon ground cinnamon

Cinammon sticks

Making potpourri

1 A day before making the potpourri, thinly peel the rind off the orange and lemon and leave it to dry in a warm place.

2 When the peel has dried, put all the ingredients for the potpourri into a bowl and mix everything together.

3 Pour the mixture into a jar, seal it, and shake it. Leave it in the jar for eight weeks and shake it every day.

POTPOURRI AND POMANDERS

And here are the scented offerings! Arrange the potpourri in a shallow bowl or on a pretty plate, and decorate it with extra sprigs of evergreen. Or put it in a potpourri box with a decorative lid. Dust any excess spice mixture off the pomanders and tie the bows neatly around them. Place them around the house where you can enjoy the scent, or wrap them in tissue paper if you are giving them as presents. As the pomanders dry out, they will shrink a little, but they will keep their scent for a year or two.

MINI POMANDER

Gold string

Kumquat

Row of cloves

Pinecone

Star anise

ORANGE POMANDER

Three rows of cloves

Green satin ribbon

POMANDERS

You can make pomanders from any citrus fruit with a thin skin. Lemon skin is too thick. Why not try making mini-pomanders from kumquats, or green ones from limes, as well as the more traditional ones, often known as clove oranges?

Gold string

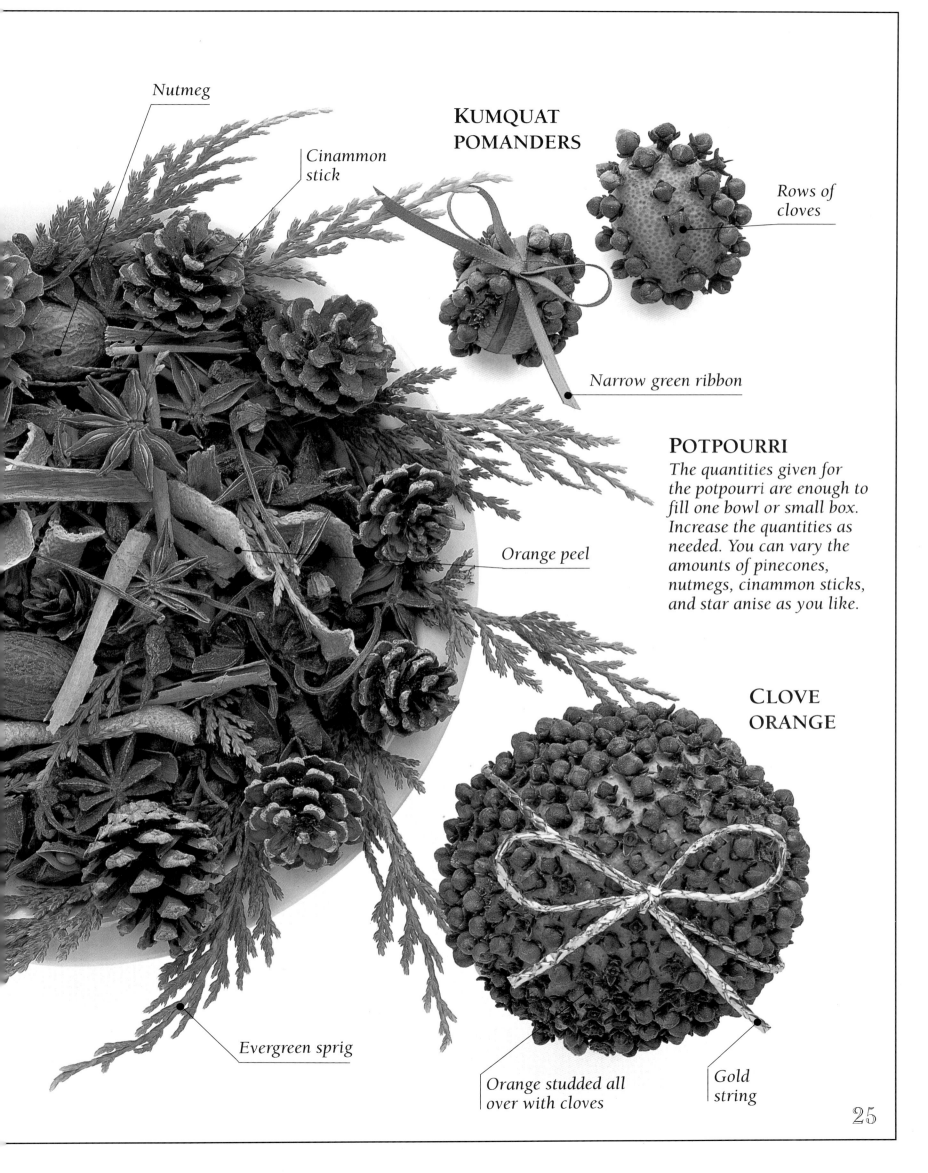

Nutmeg

Cinammon
stick

KUMQUAT
POMANDERS

Rows of
cloves

Narrow green ribbon

POTPOURRI

The quantities given for
the potpourri are enough to
fill one bowl or small box.
Increase the quantities as
needed. You can vary the
amounts of pinecones,
nutmegs, cinammon sticks,
and star anise as you like.

Orange peel

CLOVE
ORANGE

Evergreen sprig

Orange studded all
over with cloves

Gold
string

SWEET TREATS

For presents that are both scrumptious and pretty, why not make a mouthwatering array of nutty chocolate truffles and marzipan shapes? Serve them on a plate lined with shiny gold paper or wrap them in glittering boxes. The quantities given below will make about 50 large truffles and 48 marzipan shapes. Turn the page to see the finished shapes and ideas on how to wrap them.

COOK'S TOOLS *(for marzipan shapes)*

Small bowl

Fork

Mixing bowl

Cheese grater

Wooden spoon

Sharp knife

Sieve

Teaspoon

Paintbrush

You will need

Orange

Red

Green

Yellow

Pink

Brown

For marzipan shapes

A few drops of food coloring in each of these colors:

3 drops vanilla extract

1 cup (8 oz) ground almonds

½ cup (4 oz) confectioners' sugar

1 teaspoon lemon juice

1 egg and an extra egg yolk

½ cup (4 oz) superfine sugar

Pitted dates

Dried apricots

Candied cherries

Pecan or walnut halves

Cloves

COOK'S TOOLS
(for truffles)

Rolling pin

Cookie sheet

Medium saucepan

Plastic bag

4 plates

Sharp knife

Wooden spoon

For truffles

1 cup (8 oz) crumbled digestive biscuits or graham crackers

½ cup (4 oz) butter

Cocoa powder

Shredded coconut

14 oz can condensed milk

4 tablespoons shredded coconut

4 tablespoons cocoa powder

Sprinkles

Chopped nuts

26

Making the marzipan

1 Sift the confectioners' sugar into the mixing bowl. Then add the superfine sugar and the ground almonds.

2 Mix the egg, egg yolk, lemon juice, and vanilla together in the small bowl. Add them to the sugar mixture and beat well.

3 Dust the table with confectioners' sugar and gently knead the mixture until it forms a thick, smooth paste.

Stuffed fruit and nuts

1 Split the marzipan into six balls. Add coloring to five of the balls (don't use the brown coloring), and knead it in.

2 Cut the dried fruits in half, then sandwich a colored ball of marzipan between the halved dates, cherries, apricots, and nuts.

Marzipan fruit

1 For oranges, make balls of orange marzipan and roll them on a fine grater. Use cloves, head end out, to make the stalks.

2 Roll pieces of red and green marzipan together into balls to make apples. Push in a clove, head end first, to make a stem.

3 For bananas, roll pieces of yellow marzipan into banana shapes, then paint on fine lines with the brown coloring.

4 Roll green marzipan into tiny balls and press them together to make bunches of grapes. Push in cloves to make the stalks.

TRUFFLES AND BONBONS

Chocolate truffles

1 Melt the butter in a saucepan over low heat. Then remove the pan from the heat and let the butter cool slightly.

2 Break the biscuits into a plastic bag and fasten it. Then roll the rolling pin over the bag, crushing the biscuits into crumbs.

3 Add the biscuits, condensed milk, cocoa powder, and coconut to the melted butter, then mix everything together.

4 Spoon the mixture onto a buttered, shallow tin, then spread it out and level it with a spoon. Put it in the fridge to set.

5 Cut the mixture into 1 ½ in. (4 cm) squares with a knife. Then roll each square into a ball between your fingers.

6 Put the cocoa, sprinkles, nuts, and coconut on separate plates. Divide the truffles into four groups. Roll each group in a different plate.

The finished truffles

Cocoa-coated truffle

Nutty truffle

Coconut truffle

CHOCOLATE TRUFFLES

Put the truffles in candy papers. For a special Christmassy effect you can make star-shaped doilies out of shiny gold paper and arrange your truffles on them.

Gift box containing chocolate truffles and marzipan fruit

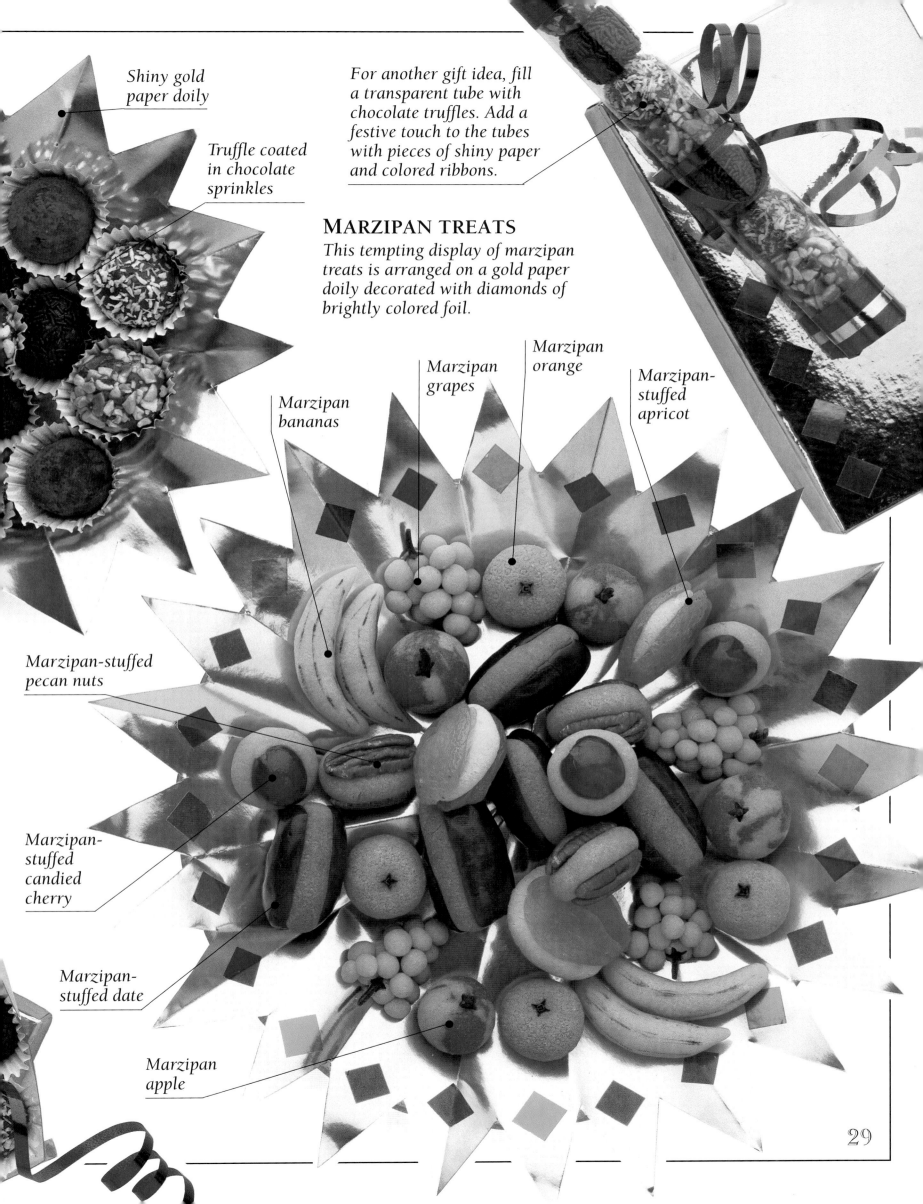

Shiny gold
paper doily

Truffle coated
in chocolate
sprinkles

For another gift idea, fill
a transparent tube with
chocolate truffles. Add a
festive touch to the tubes
with pieces of shiny paper
and colored ribbons.

MARZIPAN TREATS

This tempting display of marzipan
treats is arranged on a gold paper
doily decorated with diamonds of
brightly colored foil.

Marzipan
orange

Marzipan
grapes

Marzipan-
stuffed
apricot

Marzipan
bananas

Marzipan-stuffed
pecan nuts

Marzipan-
stuffed
candied
cherry

Marzipan-
stuffed date

Marzipan
apple

CHRISTMAS TREE DECORATIONS

The Christmas tree sparkles in its place of honor, and you can make it all the more special by making your own tree decorations. Here, you can find out how to make golden stars and bells, little Santas and snowmen, glistening icicles, a beaded garland, and tiny shining packages. Start making the decorations early in December and by Christmas you'll have enough to decorate the whole tree. Turn the page to see the festive array of finished decorations.

Rolling pin

Cookie sheet

Skewer

Sharp knife

Paintbrush

Scissors

Clear tape

You will need

For clay decorations

White and red oven-hardening clay*

Clear glaze**

Black and gold poster paint

Star and bell cookie cutters

Narrow red ribbon

For icicles

Thin wire

Clear plastic or glass beads

Small gold beads

Gold poster paint

Thick red thread

For the garland

Large and small red beads

Small pinecones

Red ribbon

For festive packages

Shiny wrapping paper

Small matchboxes

Shiny gift ribbon

**We have used acrylic polyurethane.

Clay decorations

1 Roll out the colored clays. Cut out red Santas and white bells, stars, and snowmen. Make a hole in the top of each of them.

2 Add clay details to the Santas and snowmen. Then put the cut-out clay shapes on a baking tray and harden them in the oven.*

3 Let the shapes cool. Paint the bells and stars gold and finish the snowmen's faces. Then glaze the Santas and snowmen.

Sparkling icicles

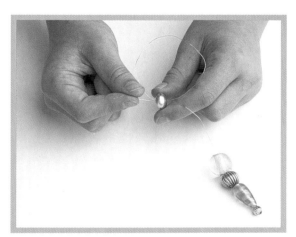

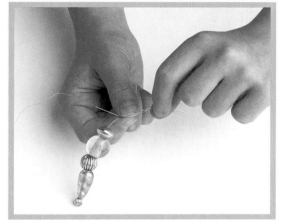

1 Thread a gold bead onto a piece of wire and fasten it by twisting the short end of the wire back around the long end.

2 Thread more beads onto the wire. Start with a clear bead, then a gold bead, and so on. Finish with a gold bead.

3 Make a hanging loop above the beads and twist the end of wire below the loop to fasten it. Trim off any extra wire.

Beaded garland

1 Paint some small pinecones with gold poster paint. Paint inside the cones as well as outside, then let them dry.

2 Knot one end of a long piece of thread, then thread beads onto it. At intervals, tie a pinecone onto the thread, between the beads.

3 Fasten the end of the garland with a knot and make hanging loops at each end. Tie ribbon bows around the pinecones.

*Ask an adult to help you harden the clay, following the instructions on the package carefully.

31

A GLITTERING TREE

The decorations are ready, and at last it is time to trim the Christmas tree. Tie each decoration firmly to a branch of the tree, making sure that each one can be seen, and that you do not hang two of the same things next to each other. Stand back from the tree from time to time to check the whole effect. Hang the sparkling icicles near the ends of the boughs, where they will catch the light. Drape the beaded garland in swags from one branch to another and add the finishing touch by tying plaid bows at the tips of the branches.

Shining boxes

1 Put a tiny gift in each matchbox. Cut out pieces of shiny paper and neatly wrap up each box. Tape the paper in place.

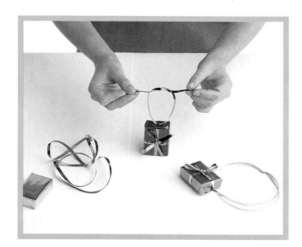

2 Tie gift ribbon around the little packages, then tie another piece of gift ribbon through each one to make a hanging loop.

Sparkling icicle

RED, GREEN, AND GOLD

Christmas trees can be a riot of different colored decorations, but they also work well if you choose a color scheme to follow. On this tree red, green, and gold have been used to create a traditional look.

PLAID BOWS

To make the tree look more dressy, tie short lengths of plaid ribbon in bows at the ends of the boughs.

Plaid bow

Shining
package

Hang the clay
decorations
with loops of
narrow red
ribbon.

Beaded
garland

Yuletide bell

Smiling
snowman

CHRISTMAS STOCKINGS

Why not make these decorative Christmas stockings for your family or friends? Fill them with tiny presents and hang them at the end of the bed for a Christmas morning surprise. The amounts of felt below will make three medium-sized stockings and all their trimmings.

EQUIPMENT

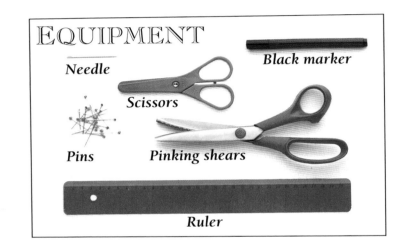

Needle

Black marker

Scissors

Pins

Pinking shears

Ruler

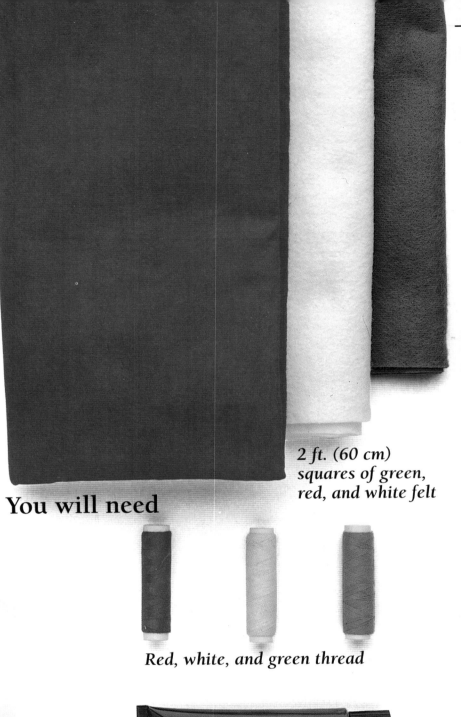

You will need

2 ft. (60 cm) squares of green, red, and white felt

Red, white, and green thread

White paper

Glue

What to do

1 Draw a stocking shape and a rectangle the same width on the paper. Cut out the paper shapes to use as patterns.

2 Pin the patterns to red and green felt. Cut out two of each shape. Cut one long side of the rectangles with pinking shears.

3 Pin the rectangles to the tops of the stocking pieces, as shown. Sew them together along the top edges.

4 Fold out the rectangular flaps. Pin and sew the two stocking pieces, right sides together, leaving the top open.

5 Turn the stocking right side out. Fold the flap down. Draw designs on felt and cut them out. Cut two felt strips to make a loop.

6 Glue your felt designs to the stocking to make a picture or pattern. For the loop, glue the two strips of felt together.

WAITING FOR SANTA

Sew the double strip of felt inside the top of the stocking to make a hanging loop. Then fill the stocking with tiny toys, candies, or other gifts and hang it on Christmas Eve.

HOLLY LEAF STOCKING

Red felt berries

Green felt holly leaves

SNOWY SANTA STOCKING

White strips of felt glued on in a zigzag pattern

Green strip cut out with pinking shears

White felt beard and moustache

Red and white felt hat

White felt dots for snow

CRACKERS

These colorful little gifts are called Christmas crackers. You may give them as holiday party favors or place them on your Christmas table as decorations. The more colors you use, the merrier!

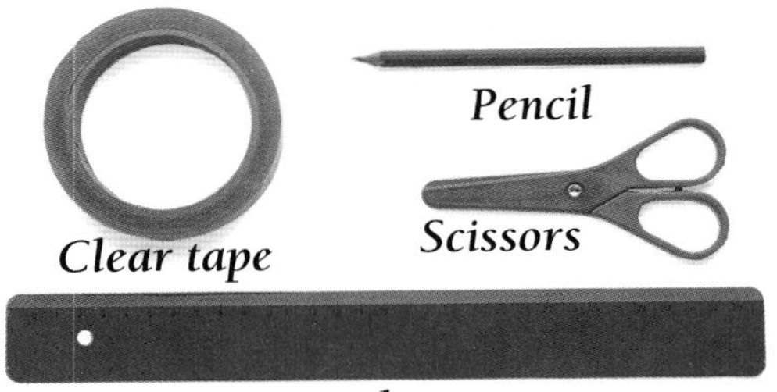

Pencil

Clear tape

Scissors

Ruler

Small cardboard tubes

You will need

Shiny gift ribbon

Shiny paper

White card for mini-crackers

Small toys or gifts

Stenciled tissue paper (see page 44)

Plain colored tissue paper

Making a cracker

1 Cut out two squares of tissue paper in different colors. Each side should be three times as long as the tube.

2 Hold the squares of paper together and cut triangles out of the top and bottom edges to make a zigzag pattern.

3 Roll the tubes up in the pieces of tissue paper and tape the top edge down. Pinch in one end of the paper.

4 Drop a small present down inside the tube and gather the tissue paper in at the other end of the cardboard tube.

5 Cut two pieces of gift ribbon in a different color than the cracker. Tie them in bows at each end of the cracker.

6 Cut out a strip of shiny paper. Wrap it around the middle of the cracker and tape it firmly in place.

PARTY CRACKERS

Give each person at your party a cracker to pull with a partner. Whoever gets the longest end wins the present inside!

Shiny wrapping paper cut with zigzag edges

Tissue paper printed with gold stars

Small gift

Mini-cracker made with a rolled-up tube of white card

GLOWING LANTERNS

Candles have long been associated with Christmas. Here you can find out how to create gilded lanterns using gold paper cutouts and colored tissue paper. Stand the finished lanterns in shadowy places and ask an adult to light them for you. Then watch your lanterns glow in the dark! Remember – never leave unattended candles burning.

You will need

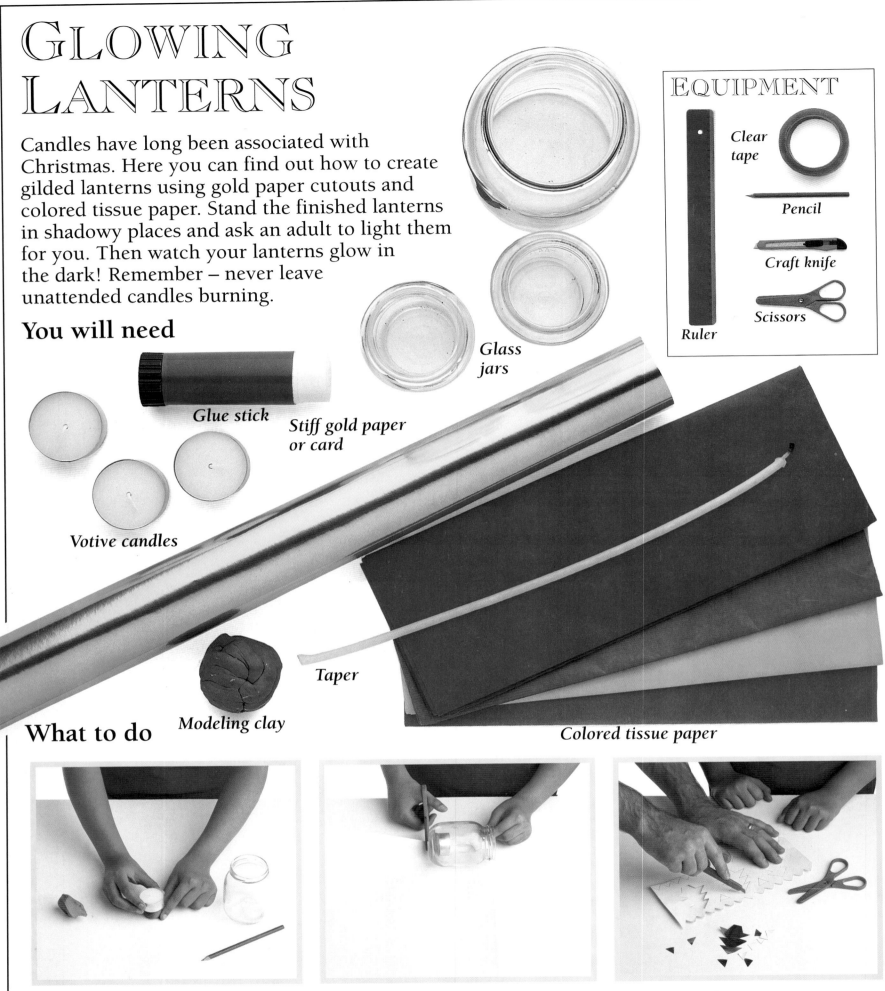

Glue stick

Stiff gold paper or card

Glass jars

Votive candles

Modeling clay

Taper

Colored tissue paper

What to do

1 Make small balls of modeling clay and push the candles into them. Put them into the jars and press them down with a pencil.

2 To make a tree or star lantern, cut a strip of gold paper wide enough to cover a jar, and long enough to wrap around it.

3 Draw a Christmassy pattern on the back of the paper and ask an adult to help you cut out the shapes with the craft knife.

38

4 Tear off pieces of colored tissue paper and glue them to the back of the gold paper, covering the cut-out patterns.

5 To make the Chinese lantern, cut a strip of gold paper taller than the jar. Fold it in half and cut slits in it, as shown.

6 To finish the lanterns, roll the patterned and decorated strips of gold paper around the jars. Tape them in place.

LIGHTS IN THE NIGHT

Stand the lanterns in a window or on a mantelpiece. Ask an adult to light them for you, using a taper.

Gold paper with slits cut in it

CHINESE LANTERN

To make the lantern more colorful, glue tissue paper to the outside of the jar before putting the gold paper around it.

STAR LANTERN

TREE LANTERN

Zigzag edges

Cut-out triangles

Cut-out Christmas tree

Cut-out diamonds

Cut-out star

39

CHRISTMAS TREE CAKE

Why not make a really special cake for Christmas? This recipe is for a delicious chocolate cake that you can transform into a dazzling Christmas tree! Iced and decorated with marzipan balls and stars, it will make a festive centerpiece for a Christmas gathering. Here you can see how to make the cake. Turn the page to find out how to decorate it.

You will need

6 large eggs

¼ cup (3½ oz) cocoa powder

1½ cups (12 oz) soft margarine

1½ cups (12 oz) self-rising flour

1½ teaspoons baking powder

A large pinch of salt

6 drops of vanilla extract

1½ cups (12 oz) superfine sugar

COOK'S TOOLS

10 in. (25 cm) square cake pan

10 in. (25 cm) square of waxed paper

Wire rack

Narrow spatula

Sharp knife

Wooden spoon

Mixing bowl

Making the cake

1 Ask and adult to help you set the oven to 325°F/170°C. Grease the cake pan and then line it with the square of waxed paper.

2 Put all the ingredients for the cake into the mixing bowl. Break the eggs into the bowl last of all.

3 Mix all the ingredients together with the wooden spoon, then beat the mixture hard for about two minutes.

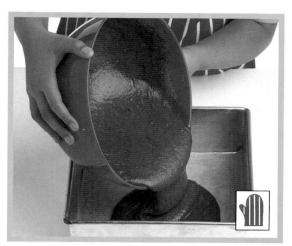

4 The cake mixture should drop off a spoon easily. If it is too stiff, stir in two teaspoons of water and stir it a bit more.

5 Pour the cake mixture into the cake pan and bake it for about 1¼ hours, or until the center feels firm and springy.

6 Let the cake cool in the pan for 30 minutes, then turn it out onto a wire rack to finish cooling and peel off the paper.

The pieces of the cake

7 When the cake is cool, cut it into the pieces shown, using a sharp knife. Start by cutting the cake in half diagonally.

Cutting the cake

The different pieces of the cake are labeled to show you how to put the cake together. There are three pieces for the tree itself, two triangles for the tree's pot, two small triangles for the star on top, and two triangles for a present standing next to the tree.

Tree 3   Tree 1   Star 1   Star 2

Pot 1

Pot 2

Present 2   Present 1   Tree 2

ICING THE CAKE

Once the cake is cool, you can ice it. Ice the pieces separately, then put them together on a big cake board, or a board covered with aluminum foil.

You will need

Yellow   Red   Green
food coloring

2 teaspoons lemon juice

½ cup (4oz) marzipan

2 egg whites

2 cups (1lb) confectioners' sugar

Apricot jam

COOK'S TOOLS

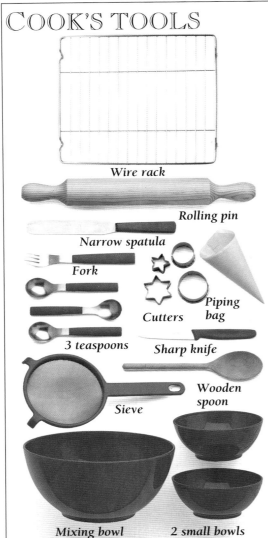

Wire rack

Rolling pin

Narrow spatula

Fork

Cutters   Piping bag

3 teaspoons   Sharp knife

Sieve   Wooden spoon

Mixing bowl   2 small bowls

What to do

1 Make the icing as on page 15. Put an eighth of it into a piping bag. Color half green, a quarter of it red, and an eighth of it yellow.

2 Spread green icing on all the pieces of the tree. Use red icing for the pot and yellow icing for the present and star.

3 When the icing has set, stick the tree together with apricot jam. Pipe zigzagging white streamers all the way down it.

4 Color half the marzipan red and half yellow. Roll it out. Cut out red circles, yellow stars, and triangles for the tree's pot.

5 Decorate the tree with the marzipan shapes as shown. Pipe on white dots and lines for the finishing touches.

The festive tree

And here is the finished tree! Use this picture for ideas of where to put the marzipan decorations and how to ice them with the white piping. Put some of the marzipan balls over the joints in the tree to help hide them.

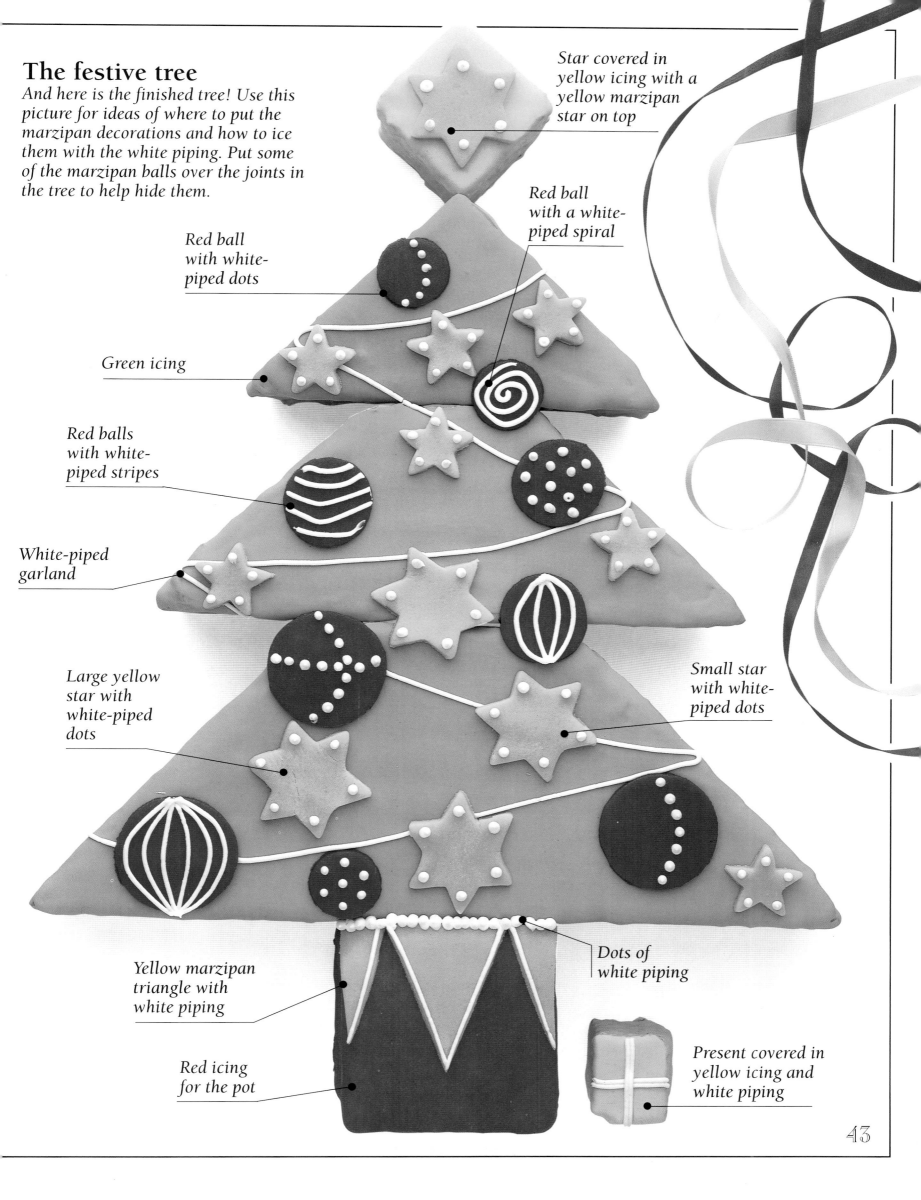

Star covered in yellow icing with a yellow marzipan star on top

Red ball with a white-piped spiral

Red ball with white-piped dots

Green icing

Red balls with white-piped stripes

White-piped garland

Large yellow star with white-piped dots

Small star with white-piped dots

Dots of white piping

Yellow marzipan triangle with white piping

Red icing for the pot

Present covered in yellow icing and white piping

Paper Workshop

You can give your Christmas presents a really personal touch by wrapping them in paper you have printed yourself. Here you can find out how to stencil paper with gold stars and angels, create bold wax and paint prints, and make gift tags. Turn the page to see how to cover your gifts with cutouts and how to wrap differently shaped presents.

You will need

Colored paper

Red and gold poster paints   *Sponge*

White paper

Thin white cardboard

Glue stick

White candle

Red and blue tissue paper

Stenciled paper

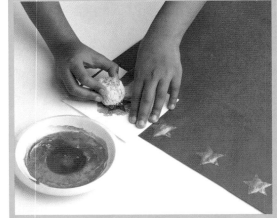

1 To make a stencil, fold a piece of card in half. Draw half a star or angel against the folded edge and cut it out. Open up the card.

2 Pour some gold paint in a saucer. Hold the stencil flat on the paper. Dab the sponge in the paint, then over the stencil shape.

3 Carefully lift the stencil off the paper. Then repeat the stencil print all over the paper to make a pattern. Leave the paper to dry.

44

Wax and paint paper

1 Draw bold patterns all over a sheet of white paper, using the white candle. Your design will be almost invisible.

2 Mix some paint with water in a saucer, then paint all over the paper as evenly as possible. Leave the paper to dry.

Gift tags

To make gift tags, cut and fold small rectangles of card. Glue on a square of wrapping paper, or make a stencil print on each one.

Print and paint

Gold star stencil on red paper

Gift tag to match the wrapping paper

Gold angel stencil on blue tissue paper

Wax and paint paper

Use strong colors so that the finished wrapping paper will look bold and make a striking effect.

UNDER WRAPS

The most inviting presents under the Christmas tree
are those that are beautifully wrapped and tied in
ribbons. Here you can find out how to wrap them
and how to decorate boxes with cutouts. Turn
the page to see the finished presents.

EQUIPMENT

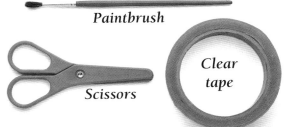

Paintbrush

Scissors

*Clear
tape*

*Colorful
ribbons*

Homemade wrapping paper

You will need

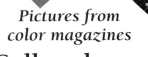

*Pictures from
color magazines*

Plain box with a lid

Glue stick

Clear glaze

Collage box

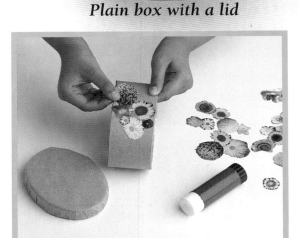

1 Cut out lots of pictures of
flowers from magazine pages.
Choose bright pictures in a range
of colors.

2 Glue the paper flowers all
around the box and lid, so
that they overlap a little and the
plain box does not show through.

3 Let the paper and glue dry
completely, then paint the
box and lid with clear glaze.
Leave them to dry.

Wrapping a rectangular present

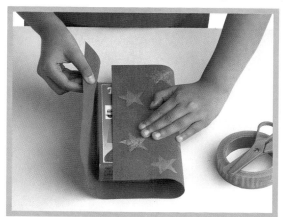

1 Put the present on a big sheet of paper. Fold the sides over the present, so they overlap. Tape them together.

2 Fold down the edge of the paper to cover one end of the present. Fold in the flaps at each side, so that they lie flat.

3 Fold in the pointed flap of paper and tape it down. Turn the present around and fold in the other end in the same way.

Wrapping a tubular present

1 Cut a long strip of paper, wider than the present. Roll the present in the paper to make a tube. Tape down the end.

2 Fold the paper down at one end of the tube. Pleat the rest of the paper down around it and tape it down.

3 Turn the tube around and fold the paper down in pleats, as before. Then tape the paper in position.

Wrapping a round present

1 Stand the present on two sheets of tissue paper. Pull the paper up over the present and cut it into a square, as shown.

2 Fold the paper up over the present and hold it with one hand. Bunch the paper in tightly and secure it with tape.

3 Cut a length of matching ribbon and cut points in the ends. Tie it over the tape in a big bow.

MERRY CHRISTMAS

And here are the finished presents! To add the last touches, tie them with ribbon and attach a gift tag to each one.

Star stenciled paper

RIBBONS AND BOWS
Tie the presents in ribbons that contrast with the wrapping paper. Some will look better with wide ribbons and others with narrow ones.

Angel stenciled tissue paper

Narrow gold ribbon

Wide gold ribbon bow

Blue box with lid decorated with cutouts

Box decorated with red and yellow cutouts

Gift tag attached with a red ribbon

Wax and paint paper with a red ribbon

Contrasting purple ribbon